Bismillahir Rahmanir Raheem
In the name of Allah the Most Gracious the Most Merciful

Everyday Islam
An Easy and Peaceful Way of Life

Shumaysa Amatul Hadi Faruqi

DJARABI KITABS PUBLISHING
Dallas, Texas

Everyday Islam
Text copyright © 2020 Shumaysa Amatul Hadi Faruqi

All rights reserved. Printed in the United States of America. No part of this book may be used or reproduced in any manner whatsoever without written permission except in the case of brief quotations embodied in critical articles or reviews.

For information contact:
DJARABI KITABS PUBLISHING
PO BOX 703733
DALLAS, TX 75370
www.djarabikitabs.com

ISBN-13: 978-1-947148-36-9
ISBN-10: 1-947148-36-2

Second Print Edition: July 2020
10 9 8 7 6 5 4 3 2 1

Table of Contents

Introduction	6
Chapter 1 This Life	10
Chapter 2 The Way of Islam	13
Chapter 3 Living Our Lives Daily	17
Waking up in the Morning	18
The Call of Nature	20
Getting Dressed	23
Having Breakfast	24
Going For Work	25
Taking a Vehicle	27
Meeting People	28
Starting Work	30
Coming Home	30
Taking Rest	32
Reading and Free Time	34

Going to the Market	37
Spending Time With Family	39
Praying	41
Socializing	44
Reading Quran	46
Fasting	47
Hajj	49
Education	52
Marriage	55
Parenting	59
Taking Care of Parents	61
Difficulties and Troubles	64
Enjoining good and Forbidding Evil	66
The Propagation of Islam	68
Summary	70
Glossary of Terms	72
Bibliography	73

Dedicated to my Parents

Late Prof. Nisar Ahmed Faruqi

Late Mrs Razia Nizami

May this book serve as an ongoing charity for them.

Introduction

All Praise is due to Allah ﷻ, Who is the Master and Owner of all that exists. I bear witness that there is only one God and that Muhammad ﷺ is His Slave and Messenger. I ask Allah to keep us guided on the straight path and to let us be among those who deserve His Pleasure and Paradise as the true Success. Amen.

Islam is a complete religion. There is no room for reframing or changing its teachings and rulings. If a believer tries, he/she can inculcate each of Islam's ways into his or her life in the most convenient manner for remaining within its fold and earning immense rewards. When a believer considers himself or herself a servant who is submissive to Allah ﷻ and His commands, he or she likes to see himself as always in obedience to Allah ﷻ. We can achieve this by learning about our religion with sincerity and devotion for implementing it in our routine lives.

Many of us live busy lives with many commitments and duties to take care of. It is highly rewarding when a Muslim remembers his Lord in all of his or her dealings in life. This is called God-consciousness, Taqwa, and it can be achieved by taking care of all of our daily situations in the light of the Quran and the traditions of the Prophet ﷺ. We must try to perform every act that we embark upon in accordance with the teachings of Islam. This is what this book is all about.

As conscious Muslims we want to always be in a state of belief and to have a chance to earn rewards, so to achieve this, we need to see our routine life and life as a whole, in the light of Islamic teachings.

From the time of waking up in the morning until the time of going to bed at night to the times of being at home and the times at the work-place, and in all of the other situations that life calls for, we can be in the state of complete submission and obedience to Allah ﷻ by learning and performing the teachings of Islam.

The following list includes some of the areas that will be discussed in this book. In shaa'Allah, I hope to help you, the reader, on an easy and peaceful journey to Islam, everyday!

1. Waking up in the morning
2. Going to the bathroom
3. Getting ready for work/school/housework etc.
4. Eating
5. Going out of the house
6. Mounting any vehicle
7. Meeting people
8. Engaging in work
9. Coming back home
10. Taking rest/ sleeping
11. Utilizing free time
12. Going to the market/park
13. Spending time with family
14. Going to the mosque/Friday prayers
15. Visiting relatives or friends/sick persons

16. Taking time to read the Quran/books
17. Fasting/celebrating festivals of Eid
18. Performing Hajj/umrah
19. Marriage
20. Child rearing
21. Taking care of parents
22. When encountering difficulties and troubles
23. Seeking knowledge
24. Enjoining good and forbidding evil
25. The Propagation of Islam

In this work the reader will be taken on a journey which brings him/her from the very start of the day and through many of the possible life situations that can occur in a general and broad sense. I'll cover the way of dealing with life situations in the Islamic way and will also present the words of Allah ﷻ and His Messenger ﷺ from the Holy Quran and the authentic Hadeeth.

The journey of *Everyday Islam: An Easy and Peaceful Way* of Life highlights the importance of living Islam in the true sense by making Islamic teachings simple and easy for identifying and implementing. The teachings of the Holy Quran and the Sunnah provide the foundation for making the practices of Islam routine in our lives.

Islam is beautiful and its wisdom is for our benefit and success. A Muslim submits himself to Allah ﷻ and makes Islam his identity and his priority in every situation. I am hoping and praying that this work is accepted in the way of Allah ﷻ and that Allah ﷻ may cause it to benefit all the

Muslim brothers and sisters who love Islam and want to see it shining in their life here in the world, and causing them to shine in the Hereafter.

-Shumaysa Faruqi, July 2014

Chapter 1 This Life

Allah the Exalted has created us to live on this earth in a better manner than the rest of His creations. Man has been created with a better understanding and intelligence than all the other creations of Allah on earth.

Allah says in Surah Al Balad of the Holy Quran:
Have We not given him two eyes,
and a tongue and two lips,
and shown him both the highways (of good and evil)? (8-10)

And in Surah At Tin:
Verily, We created man of the best stature (moulds) (4)

Life exists in the minutest of Allah's ﷻ creations but man has been given much more than just survival techniques. Apart from the senses of hearing, sight, smell, taste and touch; man has the ability to understand, think, reason, calculate, talk and much more. The intelligence of man has surprised man himself!

We often talk about the various inventions of man like the telephone, radio, computer etc. and wonder at the way they were invented. This was made possible because of the intelligence that has been bestowed on man by his Lord.

Allah says in Surah Al Alaq (Iqra):
He Who taught (the use of) the pen,-

Taught man that which he knew not. (4-5)

Allah ﷻ has sent us onto this earth and we should ponder over the visible signs of Allah ﷻ and believe in our Unseen Creator who watches us all the time.

In Surah Dhariyat of the Holy Quran it reads:

> *And on the earth are signs for the certain [in faith]*
> *And in yourselves. Then will you not see? (20-21)*

Living on this earth may become complicated if we get lost in the worldly pleasures alone, like the luxuries of life, the facilities that exist, longing for things, and the ties of love and relationships. Anas bin Malik رضي الله عنه reported:

> *Messenger of Allah (ﷺ) said, "Among the inmates of Hell, a person who had led the most luxurious life in this world will be brought up on the Day of Resurrection and dipped in the Fire and will be asked:*
>
> *'O son of Adam! Did you ever experience any comfort? Did you happen to get any luxury?' He will reply: 'By Allah, no, my Rubb.' And then one of the people of Jannah who had experienced extreme misery in the life of this world will be dipped in Jannah. Then he will be asked:*
>
> *'O son of Adam! Did you ever experience any misery? Did you ever encounter difficulty?' He will say: "By Allah, no my*

Rubb, I neither experienced misery nor passed through hardship". [Muslim].

It is obvious that when one lives in such a world where there is always one or the other thing happening, the person might get confused and lost. But our Lord, the Most Merciful has not created us to leave us in such a state. He has bestowed upon us His Book and His Messenger for showing us how we can live on this earth the way He wants us to. In Surah Al Baqarah verse 120 it is stated:

> ...Say, "Indeed, the guidance of Allah is the [only] guidance."...

That way is the Way of Islam. Islam is not just a religion but a complete layout or a lifestyle to be followed. It is the religion of our beloved Prophet Muhammed ﷺ and of all the other Prophets that came before him ﷺ.

In Surah Ali Imran verse 85 Allah ﷻ says:

> "And whoever desires other than Islam as religion - never will it be accepted from him, and he, in the Hereafter, will be among the losers."

Chapter 2 The Way of Islam

The way of Islam is easy and peaceful if one tries to follow it accordingly. The Holy Quran and the traditions and sayings of the Prophet Muhammed ﷺ are the fundamental resources that every Muslim needs when seeking to follow this way. It is recorded in the sayings of the Prophet ﷺ as follows:

> 'Ali reported that one day Allah's Messenger (ﷺ) was sitting with a wood in his hand and he was scratching the ground. He raised his head and said:
> There is not one amongst you who has not been allotted his seat in Paradise or Hell. They said: Allah's Messenger, then, why should we perform good deeds, why not depend upon our destiny? Thereupon he said. No, do perform good deeds, for everyone is facilitated in that for which he has been created; then he recited this verse:" Then, who gives to the needy and guards against evil and accepts the excellent (the truth of Islam and the path of righteousness it prescribes), We shall make easy for him the easy end..." (xcii. 5-10). Sahih Muslim 2647 c

Our prophet Muhammed ﷺ is a human being from amongst us. He is chosen for us. Therefore we can easily identify with him. We can be reassured by the fact that the Prophet Muhammed ﷺ was a human being who was able to follow what Allah ordered him, so why can't we try?

Surah Al Baqarah 112 reads:

> ...whoever submits his face in Islam to Allah while being a doer of good will have his reward with his Lord. And no fear will there be concerning them, nor will they grieve.

It is understandable to feel that our Prophet ﷺ is the chosen one and the blessed one, so it was easy for him to follow Allah ﷻ. We are weak, sinning and faulty, so how can we follow Islam the same way? It has been narrated by Anas bin Malik ﷺ :

> *A group of three men came to the houses of the wives of the Prophet (ﷺ) asking how the Prophet (ﷺ) worshipped (Allah), and when they were informed about that, they considered their worship insufficient and said, "Where are we from the Prophet (ﷺ) as his past and future sins have been forgiven." Then one of them said, "I will offer the prayer throughout the night forever." The other said, "I will fast throughout the year and will not break my fast." The third said, "I will keep away from the women and will not marry forever." Allah's Messenger (ﷺ) came to them and said, "Are you the same people who said so-and-so? By Allah, I am more submissive to Allah and more afraid of Him than you; yet I fast and break my fast, I do sleep and I also marry women. So he who does not follow my tradition in religion, is not from me (not one of my followers). Sahih Al Bukhari 5063*

We must not forget that our Prophet ﷺ set an example in everything for us to follow. Allah ﷻ guided him in his affairs so that the Muslims could understand the religion and follow it in the best manner. Another hadith tradition reads:

> *Abu Hurayra ﷺ reported that the Messenger of Allah, may Allah bless him and grant him peace, said, "I was sent to perfect good character."*
> Sahih Al Albani

And in Surah Al Qalam verse 4 of the Holy Quran Allah ﷻ tells the Prophet Muhammad ﷺ:

And indeed, you are of a great moral character.

For us it is important to understand that we must not make things hard rather choose the easy and uncomplicated path. This is what our Prophet (peace and blessings of Allah be upon him) has guided us to do.

Another hadith narration by Abu Huraira ﺭﺿﻲ ﺍﻟﻠﻪ ﻋﻨﻪ states:

The Prophet ﷺ said, "Religion is very easy and whoever overburdens himself in his religion will not be able to continue in that way. So you should not be extremists, but try to be near to perfection and receive the good tidings that you will be rewarded; and gain strength by worshipping in the mornings, the nights." (See Fath-ul-Bari, Page 102, Vol 1). Sahih Al Bukhari 39

There is always the room for trying and this effort in the way of Islam is what is liked by Allah ﷻ. We can try to be like our Prophet ﷺ in whatever we do. We can adopt his ways of doing things and feel closer and deeper in Islam which is undoubtedly the best way of life. It is in fact quite a natural tendency in man to try to achieve excellence in his capabilities and to utilize all the skills that he has to live a successful and prosperous life. To Muslims, this life is not just one way but rather it is a complete way but only if we strive for both this world and the world hereafter while keeping our connection with the Creator.

When trying to do things the way our Prophet ﷺ did, we not only head toward a better life but we also earn enormous reward in this venture.

Chapter 3 Living Our Lives Daily

One might wonder how to give life a complete meaning and how to achieve the station of reward, but as mentioned earlier, God did not leave us unguided. We have been given a detailed account for all walks of life through the example of our Last Prophet Muhammad ﷺ. If a Muslim wants to lead a life loved by Allah ﷻ he or she has to follow the example of the Prophet ﷺ, and to achieve this he has to gain knowledge in this regard. When we come to know 'what' we are supposed to do we can take a step forward in learning 'how' we need to achieve it.

Gaining knowledge about the way of life recommended by the Holy Quran and Sunnah is the only successful way and this is Islam. How can we give it a start? We can start right from the moment we wake up in the morning, keeping in mind the ways of our Prophet ﷺ as we proceed with our daily routine and rituals. What did our Prophet ﷺ do when he woke up in the morning? What did he say? How did he proceed toward his daily duties?

Once we get the answers to these questions and start implementing them one by one we will, in shaa'Allah, get used to these routines and they will not feel even a bit unfamiliar once we add them to the things that we incorporate in our lives. Some of the daily rituals of life that are broadly the same for everyone are waking up in the morning, going to the bathroom, getting ready for work/school/housework etc., eating, going out of the house, mounting any vehicle, meeting people, engaging in work, coming back home, taking rest/ sleeping, utilizing free time, spending time with family, going to the mosque/Friday prayers, visiting relatives or friends/sick persons, taking time to read the Quran/books, fasting/celebrating festivals of Eid, performing Hajj/umrah, marriage, child rearing, taking care of parents, enduring difficulties and troubles, seeking knowledge, enjoining good, forbidding evil and the propagation of Islam.

These are some of the daily situations that each one of us embark upon or go through at some point in time. All of the above mentioned activities can be carried out while keeping in mind the ways of our Prophet Muhammad ﷺ. Let us now see how we can go about these activities while implementing the example of our Prophet ﷺ for earning rewards from Allah ﷻ. Let us see how we can easily incorporate some Islamic practices into our life and make them daily habits.

Waking up in the morning:

Our beloved Prophet Muhammad ﷺ used to wake up early in the morning and he used to recite the following supplication mentioned in the Hadeeth:

> Hudhaifah ؓ reported:
> Whenever the Prophet (ﷺ) lay down for sleep at night, he would place his (right) hand under his (right) cheek and supplicate: "Allahumma bismika amutu wa ahya [O Allah, with Your Name will I die and live (wake up)]." And when he woke up, he would supplicate: "Al-hamdu lillahil-ladhi ahyana ba'da ma amatana, wa ilaihin-nushur (All praise is due to Allah, Who has brought us back to life after He has caused us to die, and to Him is the return)." Al-Bukhari

Abu Huraira ؓ reported:

> *The Apostle of Allah ﷺ said: When anyone amongst you wakes up from sleep, he should wash his hands three times before putting it in the utensil, for he does not know where his hand was during the night.*
> *Sahih Muslim*

Our Prophet Muhammad ﷺ used Miswak after waking up, he made wudhu or ghusl and performed the Sunnah of Fajr prayers at home, and then left for the Masjid to offer the obligatory congregational prayer. He taught us that one should dress up neatly and completely to go to the Masjid. He has also been said to have revealed that whosoever prays the Fajr prayer finds a happy morning otherwise laziness and misfortune find him. It is known that sleeping until late in the morning is unhealthy for us and so we, as Muslims, can feel proud deep in our hearts as we sincerely seek to attain a good lifestyle according to how our Prophet ﷺ has guided us.

We must never be irresponsible toward our first morning prayer, i.e., the Fajr prayer and there are ways to make it a habit to wake up for the Fajr prayer. We should sleep early after Isha prayers and should not stay awake late into the night if we really wish to wake up for Fajr. First, we can sleep with the intention of waking up for Fajr and then we must make sure that we wake up with the help of some person or alarm clock. It is very sad that we can keep an alarm for an early morning meeting or other events but not for the spiritual head start that we need for all of our ventures.

Imagine the consequences of not starting something right. How can we expect the best results at the end of the day? So it is best to first become really serious and responsible about making the first prayer of the day which is very important for us.

It was narrated that Abu Hurairah said:

> "The Messenger of Allah ﷺ said: 'At night Satan ties a rope in which there are three knots to the nape of the neck of anyone of you. If he wakes up and remembers Allah, one knot is untied. If he performs ablution, another knot is untied, and if he gets up to pray, all the knots are untied, so he wakes up energetic and cheerful, he has already earned something good. But if he does not do that, he wakes up bad-tempered, having earned nothing good."
> Sahih Sunan ibn Majah

The Call of Nature

After waking up and using the siwak we normally need to go to the bathroom. There is a very short and easy supplication for entering the bathroom:

Narrated Anas:

> Whenever the Prophet ﷺ went to answer the call of nature, he used to say, "Allah-umma inni a'udhu bika minal khubuthi wal khaba'ith i.e. O Allah, I seek Refuge with You from all offensive and wicked things (evil deeds and evil spirits).

This supplication renders us safe from the evil creatures. Abu Huraira reported:

> The Messenger of Allah ﷺ said: When anyone performs ablution he must clean his nose and when anyone wipes himself with pebbles (after answering the call of nature) he must do that odd number of times.

After coming out we are advised to say: *ghufraanaka, alhamdulillahil ladhi adhhaba anil aadha wa aafaani.*

This means that we are thanking Allah ﷻ for saving us and for giving us relief from uncomfortable/painful things.

While in the bathroom there should be screening from others and one should not talk unnecessarily and we must take care to protect our bodies and clothing from getting soiled by urine or feces. It is important that we clean ourselves properly and take regular baths to avoid bad odors. Cleanliness is part of faith and one should be very particular about keeping oneself clean all the time.

When we take a bath we should keep in mind the appropriate way for doing so and must avoid wasting a lot of water and taking too much time in the bathroom. We should also take a bath according to the Sunnah., as it is written, Allah ﷻ loves those who purify themselves.

Narrated Maimuna:

The Prophet ﷺ took the bath of Janaba. (sexual relation or wet dream). He first cleaned his private parts with his hand, and then rubbed it (that hand) on the wall (earth) and washed it. Then he performed ablution like that for the prayer, and after the bath he washed his feet.

As excess in everything is discouraged in Islam, we see the example to the Messenger using an adequate amount of water to perform Ghusl or bath as important. It was narrated from 'Aishah that:

The Messenger of Allah ﷺ used to perform Ghusl with a Mudd and Ghusl with approximately a Sa'. Sahih Sunan an Nisai

It is indeed very empowering to know that Allah ﷻ loves those who keep themselves pure and clean. This purity is both physical and spiritual, and constant efforts are needed for them to be achieved.

Surah At Tauba 108 reads:
and Allah loves those who purify themselves.

Allah ﷻ has even explained to us the way to perform the ablution for prayer in the Holy Quran and we have the perfect guidance through the Book as well as in the example of our Prophet ﷺ in every matter of Faith.

Surah Al Maidah 6 reads:

> *O you who have believed, when you rise to [perform] prayer, wash your faces and your forearms to the elbows and wipe over your heads and wash your feet to the ankles. And if you are in a state of janabah, then purify yourselves. But if you are ill or on a journey or one of you comes from the place of relieving himself or you have contacted women and do not find water, then seek clean earth and wipe over your faces and hands with it. Allah does not intend to make difficulty for you, but He intends to purify you and complete His favor upon you that you may be grateful.*

Cleanliness is comprised of much more than mere wudhu or a bath. If we take proper care of our hair, keep ourselves clean and well groomed then we will be following the Sunnah. Our Prophet ﷺ used to keep his hair neatly combed and oiled. We need to clip our nails and keep them clean of dirt. Men can apply perfume to smell good. Women can also apply perfume but should not go out wearing it as it is forbidden. The Prophet used to smell so nice that no one had ever smelled any perfume better than his perfume.

Getting Dressed

After taking a bath we usually dress up for work. Our beloved Prophet ﷺ used to recite a supplication while dressing up:

> "alhamdolillahil ladhi kasaani ma uwaari bihi aurati wa atajammalu bihi fi hayaati"

In this dua one praises the Lord for providing clothing which protects and beautifies us in our life. The following Hadith tells us the Sunnah way of wearing Izar or a lower garment.

Narrated Abu Huraira:

> The Prophet ﷺ said, "The part of an Izar which hangs below the ankles is in the Fire."
> Sahih Bukhari 5787

He also advised us to always put the right arm or leg first while putting on a shirt or pants and to take out the left arm or leg first while taking off clothes. This goes for wearing shoes as well.

Narrated ʿAisha:

> The Prophet ﷺ used to like to start from the right side on wearing shoes, combing his hair and cleaning or washing himself and on doing anything else.
> Sahih Al Bukhari 168

One should first check the shoes then wear the right shoe first and then the left. When taking off the shoes the left shoe is taken off first and then the right one. Every action has its benefits in Islam. It is possible that if we do not check that the shoes are clean we might get bitten or stung by an insect which may have crawled inside our shoes during the night. Starting all good things from the right side and saying bismillah is something that brings barakah into actions.

Having Breakfast

Now before leaving for work we usually have breakfast. Whenever we eat or drink, the first thing we must do is to say *Bismillahi wa ala barakatillah* which means 'In the name of Allah and with the blessings of Allah." This ensures that there is barakah in our food and that Shaitan does not share this food with us, hence we will be getting the benefit out of what we eat. Also, saying bismillah over food before eating makes it *halaal* or permitted for us. Allah ﷻ also instructs us to eat from the good things that He has given us.

Surah Al Baqarah 172 states:
> *O you who have believed, eat from the good things which We have provided for you and be grateful to Allah if it is [indeed] Him that you worship.*

We must not overstuff ourselves and should rather eat sensibly to gain strength and stamina. Milk, honey, vegetables, meat, fruits and grains are good for health if we include them in our diets according to our needs. The Messenger of Allah ﷺ used to eat in moderation and never criticized any food.

He used to eat in the sitting position like a slave sits before his master.

We as the followers of Islam should reflect on our attitudes toward food. Do we regard food as our target in life? Do we find ourselves always ready to grab tasty food and start enjoying it whether we feel hungry or not? We must read the history of Islam and see how the early Muslims lived without proper food for days and months just for the sake of Allah ﷻ. They were not greedy for food but they ate food to keep themselves alive and to gain some strength to fight for the cause of Allah ﷻ and to spread Islam. We should eat food with the intention of gaining health and vitality and not for gluttony and greed.

The hadith states:

"The believer eats with one intestine and the disbeliever eats with seven intestines.'"
Sahih Ibn Majah

The manners of eating food have been reported in many Ahadith and advise us to be self-disciplined and well-mannered even when the tastiest of foods are in front of our eyes!

Narrated Abdullah ibn Abbas:

The Prophet ﷺ said: When one of you eats, he must not eat from the top of the dish, but should eat from the bottom; for the blessing descends from the top of it. Sahih Al Albani

Going Out for Work

Narrated Al-Aswad bin Yazid:

I asked `Aisha "What did the Prophet ﷺ use to do at home?" She said, "He used to work for his family, and when he heard the Adhan (call for the prayer), he would go out." Sahih Al Bukhari 5363

Upon finishing with food we usually intend to go out for work or study. We greet our family members before leaving and in Islam, the best greeting while meeting or leaving someone is *Assalaam Alaikum Wa Rahmahtullahi Wa Barakahtuhu* which means may the peace, blessings and mercy of Allah be upon you. Surah An Nisa 86 reads:

And when you are greeted with a greeting, greet [in return] with one better than it or [at least] return it [in a like manner]. Indeed, Allah is ever, over all things, an Accountant.

This greeting not only instills love and respect among Muslims but also gives us tremendous reward. Before leaving we should greet our family in this manner and then leave the house saying *"bismillahi tawakkaltu alal laahi wa la haula wa la quwwata illa billah,"* which means that we have invoked Allah for his blessing and for His protection from the Shaitan.

When the spouse leaves the house it is good that he or she give each other a handshake or hug and kiss each other. This will increase the love and bonding between them. It is always good to keep a strong bond between husband and wife and to stay connected to each other so that there is not much room for misunderstanding and longing for each other's company.

It was narrated that Aisha, said:

"Some Bedouin people came to the Prophet ﷺ and said: 'Do you kiss your children?' He said: 'Yes'. He said: 'But we, by Allah, never kiss (our children)'. The Prophet ﷺ said: 'What can I do if Allah has taken away mercy from you?'" Sunan Ibn Majah

Being kind and merciful to children and to other family members is highly recommended. When the head of the house leaves with a smile, with hugs and kisses to his family he will leave with a tranquil and thankful heart and he will leave them with the same. He is going out for fulfilling his duty of providing for the family; hence he needs that positive outlook and calmness to deal with the stress at the work place. The wife and children and other members too need a good environment to bring out the best in them while they do their part at home, at school or at work.

Taking a Vehicle

We usually take some sort of vehicle, like a car, a bus, or a taxi to reach the work place or school. While entering a car or any other vehicle we should say the supplication for travelling, *"subhanal ladhi sakhkharalana haaza wama kunna lahu muqrineen, wa inna ila rabbina la munqalibun."* This is translated to mean, "Praise be to Allah Glory unto to Him who has subjected this (vehicle) for us, though we were unable to subdue it. Behold we are assuredly to return unto our Lord."

This supplication comes to us from the Quran itself in Surah Az Zukhruf 13:

That you may settle yourselves upon their backs and then remember the favor of your Lord when you have settled upon them and say, "Exalted is He who has subjected this to us, and we could not have [otherwise] subdued it.

This ensures our safety and the help of Allah ﷻ throughout our travels. Even if we walk to our workplace, school or college we can say any of the supplications which are easy on our tongues and heavy in reward like: *subhaanal laahi wa bihamdihi subhaanal laahil azeem*, which means glorified is Allah and praised is He, glorified is Allah the Most Great; *la haula wa la quwwata illa billah*, which means there is no power or strength except with Allah; or *astaghfirullah*, meaning I ask Allah's forgiveness or any short dua or Allah's ﷻ beautiful names that we wish to recite.

This will give us tremendous reward and we will also feel peace within. Saying our supplications starting from the morning supplications to the supplications of protection and forgiveness, and for healing gives us a great sense of confidence and trust in Allah ﷻ. We find ourselves under the merciful protection of Allah ﷻ all the time. He protects us from calamities, accidents and mishaps and even if it is meant to happen then we are not at a loss because we have been in the shield of Allah's ﷻ protection and have remembered Him which is enough for us to feel fortunate.

On the contrary, if we keep busy in everything and do not care about saying our daily supplications we might find ourselves ungrateful as well as unsafe in adverse circumstances. It is always good to be in Allah's ﷻ remembrance with our actions, our tongues and our hearts. Being conscious of Allah

ﷺ is a part of faith and doing so all the time is truly encouraging and helpful in our day to day business.

Meeting People

As we reach our destination we meet many people. Jabir has said in Sahih Al Albani, "When two people walking meet, then the one who gives the greeting first is the better of them."

Again, the best manners are to greet our Muslim brothers and sisters with the Islamic greeting, but we must not ignore non-Muslim individuals. We can greet them with the appropriate greeting like good morning or how do you do and when meeting others a smile is also a charity.

Abu Dharr narrated that the Messenger of Allah ﷺ said:

"Your smiling in the face of your brother is charity, commanding good and forbidding evil is charity, your giving directions to a man lost in the land are charity for you. Your seeing for a man with bad sight is a charity for you, your removal of a rock, a thorn or a bone from the road is charity for you. Your pouring what remains from your bucket into the bucket of your brother is charity for you."
Jami At Tirmidhi Hasan

It bears great reward. Be it at a Muslim or a non-Muslim person, a young or an old person, or a rich or poor person. We should be meeting others in a pleasant manner. This ensures a peaceful and harmonious environment and plants seeds of love and respect for Muslims in the hearts of others.

Abu Dharr reported:

Allah's Apostle ﷺ said to me: Don't consider anything insignificant out of good things even if it is that you meet your brother with a cheerful countenance. Sahih Muslim 2626

Starting Work

When we start with any work we should not forget to say the In the Name of Allah in the beginning. Saying *Bismillah* at the beginning of any work is recommended so that Allah ﷻ will bless our work and makes it easy for us to achieve success in it. Doing any good work, like any office project, school work, physical work, or examination requires our full sincerity and devotion. We must take our responsibilities seriously during work. Being sincere and hardworking brings success and reward in that venture in shaa'Allah.

Muslims are discouraged to beg others and are encouraged to work hard for sustaining themselves and their families. From the hadith below we are clearly advised to take up even the most menial of jobs to provide for ourselves and family and not to ask of others. We should work hard, take action, do our best and leave the rest in the hands of Allah ﷻ.

Narrated Abu Huraira:

Allah's Messenger ﷺ said, "By Him in Whose Hand my life is, it is better for anyone of you to take a rope and cut the wood (from the forest) and carry it over his back and sell it (as a means of earning his living) rather than to ask a person for something and that person may give him or not." Sahih Bukhari 1470

Coming Home

When our work finishes we head back to our homes. Coming back home is refreshing and relaxing. While entering the house we should say *bismillahi walajna wa bismillahi kharajna, wa ila rabbina tawakkalna*, which means that by Allah's name we go out and enter and on Him do we put our trust.

As we enter the house we should greet the family members so that they are informed of our arrival and wish them peace as a greeting. It is nice to talk to the spouse and kids and other relatives in a cheerful and happy tone and spend light moments in their company. This makes the environment in the house comfortable and relaxing.

Helping out in the housework is also a very good way to interact with the family and make the bond stronger among the members. In this regard we must see the example of our beloved Prophet ﷺ who used to help out in the housework and stay with his family to spend time with them. When the time of prayer arrived the Prophet ﷺ used to set out for performing his duty toward Allah ﷻ.

Hisham ibn 'Urwa said that his father said, "I asked 'A'isha, may Allah be pleased with her, 'What did the Prophet ﷺ do in his house?' She replied, 'He mended his sandals and worked as any man works in his house.'" *Sahih Al Albani*

Taking Rest

After much work and chores one needs to take rest for a while. It is better if one takes a light nap after having lunch.

Narrated Anas bin Malik:
We used to offer the Jumua prayer early and then have an afternoon nap. Sahih Al Bukhari 905

It is good for us to take rest so that our body feels revitalized, but too much sleep during the day makes one lazy. A nap just after lunch is very refreshing even if it is for 10 minutes or even less because we tire our bodies from the various tasks at home and work. Our bodies need to relax and regain strength to continue with other tasks. Sleep is the best way to give this strength back to the body because our nervous system and the overall body systems relax during sleep.

With regard to the afternoon nap which is called siesta, according to Enric Zamorano, the coordinator of the Mental Health and Sleep working group from SEMERGEN, research states that a siesta should be taken for a short time and without entering deep sleep because otherwise one may not be able to sleep at night.

New Spanish recommendations follow findings by the American space agency NASA which found that the optimum length of a nap is 26 minutes. The recent NASA study showed that when pilots were allowed to take a nap for 26 minutes during their working hours, their efficiency increased by 34 per cent.

Apart from taking rest in the afternoon a good sleep in the night is even more refreshing and healthy. A good sleep keeps our mind, body and soul in a good condition. Just as our beloved

Prophet peace be upon him, guided us by the Will of Allah in every small and big matter he gave us instructions regarding the night sleep as well.

He used a simple and hard surface for sleeping. He did not like cushioning his bed so much so that he slept through the Tahajjud (midnight prayer) or Fajr prayers (morning prayer). He was moderate in his sleeping patterns. He did not sleep too much or too little in the night. He instructed to say Bismillah and close the doors of the house, cover the utensils and put off the lights before going to bed.

Narrated Abu Barza:

Allah's Messenger ﷺ disliked to sleep before the 'Isha' prayer and to talk after it.
Sahih Bukhari 568

It was disliked to stay up till late into the night and indulge in useless stories and activities. Another tradition states in Al-Bukhari and Muslim that the Messenger of Allah ﷺ disliked going to bed before the 'Isha' (night) prayer and indulging in conversation after it."

Our Prophet Muhammad ﷺ used to clean his bed before reclining for sleep. He also ordered the kids to be taken in as the night fell and he used to do miswak (toothbrush) before sleeping, and after waking up in the morning. In addition, the Prophet ﷺ always slept while in Wudu (in the state of purity by ablutions) turning to the right side of his body, as it is disliked to sleep on one's stomach, and he put his right palm under his cheek or head.

Some of the supplications that he recited before sleeping include the last three Chapters of the Holy Quran (Surah Ikhlas, Surah Falaq and Surah An Nas), Surah Mulk and some other parts of the Holy Quran. One of the supplications to recite before going to sleep is, *"Allahumma bismika amautu wa ahya,"* which means, *"O Allah with Your Name I die and I live."*

Lastly, it is recommended to wash the hands soon after waking up before putting them into any vessel or using things.

Reading and Free Time

Most of our time these days passes in worldly affairs. For many, the only time we remember Allah ﷻ is during prayers and that too can sometimes be mechanical and void of real devotion. We must work on this. This takes some effort but it is worthwhile. We should take some time out daily to read some portion of the Quran. We can also have our children sit with us and read Quran with Tajweed (the correct way of reciting the Quran) while explaining the meaning for at least 10 minutes.

It is very fruitful to make kids listen to stories of Prophets and the Miracles of Allah ﷻ and those given to His prophets. Children enjoy these kinds of talks and tales. We can read useful and informative books. We can surf the net for important information on topics that concern us like health, Islam, science, nature, general knowledge on authentic websites.

We can utilize our free time in going out to different places and visiting family friends and relatives. It is also nice to take interest in learning the skills of swimming, horse riding, calligraphy, and others. There are numerous ways to use one's time intelligently and constructively.

Allah likes strong Muslims better than those who do not take care of themselves and are weak and unproductive.

It was narrated that Abu Hurairah said:

"The Messenger of Allah ☐ said: 'The strong believer is better and more beloved to Allah than the weak believer, although both are good. Strive for that which will benefit you, seek the help of Allah, and do not feel helpless. If anything befalls you, do not say, "if only I had done such and such" rather say "Qaddara Allahu wa ma sha'a fa'ala (Allah has decreed and whatever he wills, He does)." For (saying) 'If' opens (the door) to the deeds of Satan.'"
Sahih Sunan Ibn Majah

Utilizing our time in a productive manner will not only benefit us personally but also make us beneficial for our family and others. We as Muslims know that whatever good deeds we do are immensely rewarding. No minor deed is worthless. Making ourselves more and more useful and beneficial for others is our contribution to the world and Afterlife. Our children will learn from our behavior and they too will act responsibly toward being useful and not wasting their time, energy and skills. The good deeds will act like ongoing charity if we have started something for the good of others and it will keep benefiting us even after we have left the world.

What more do we need for a better life and a successful end?! This is not limited to some specific day or time rather this should be there in our hearts every day. We are not Muslims only when we pray or fast or perform other duties. We are Muslims every moment that we utilize according to what Allah likes and keeping a constant check on ourselves whether we are fulfilling our duties in every aspect of life. This is because Islam is not just a label or a cult but it is a lifestyle and a code of conduct for daily life.

Going to the Marketplace

We need to buy things for the house so we go out to the market. For the ladies it is best to wear a hijab when going out and for the gents to guard their gaze.

Surah An Nur 31

And tell the believing women to lower their gaze (from looking at forbidden things), and protect their private parts (from illegal sexual acts, etc.) and not to show off their adornment except only that which is apparent (like palms of hands or one eye or both eyes for necessity to see the way, or outer dress like veil, gloves, head-cover, apron, etc.), and to draw their veils all over Juyubihinna (i.e. their bodies, faces, necks and bosoms, etc.) and not to reveal their adornment except to their husbands, their fathers, their husband's fathers, their sons, their husband's sons, their brothers or their brother's sons, or their sister's sons, or their (Muslim) women (i.e. their sisters in Islam), or the (female) slaves whom their right hands possess, or old male servants who lack vigor, or small children who have no sense of the shame of sex. And let them not stamp their feet so as to reveal what they hide of their adornment. And all of you beg Allah to forgive you all, O believers, that you may be successful.

It is highly beneficial for the believing ladies to dress themselves modestly whenever they go out of their houses.
The scenario today is of an unprotected world with almost every other person exposed to the ills of immorality and shamelessness. The media and other networks have made the viewers have easy access to obscene and vulgar things. Even if someone does not want to see anything objectionable he is forced to come in contact with it through various channels like magazines, newspapers, products in the market and internet sites and advertisements and bill boards! In such a situation when we

are prone to information which we should be avoiding the only solution left is to adhere to the teachings of Quran and Sunnah and to abstain from such shameful things which incite undesirable emotions and behavior toward unrelated men and women.

While entering the market one must remember Allah and say, *la ilaaha illallaahu wahdahu la shareeka lahu lahul mulku wa lahul hamdu yuhyi wa yamutu wa hua ala kulli shayin qadeer* which means None has the right to be worshipped except Allaah, alone, without partner, to Him belong all sovereignty and praise, He gives life and causes death and He is over all things Omnipotent.

When one reads this Allah protects him from the shaytan's whisperings and gives him profit in his dealings Inshaa'Allah. Also it is highly praised when one remembers Allah in a market because market is one of the favorite places for shaytan as he gets chances to deviate a Muslim from the right path guiding him toward greed and the desires to possess things. The most liked places for Allah are the Masajids (mosques) and the disliked ones are the market places.

Abu Huraira reported that the Messenger of Allah ﷺ said:

> *The parts of land dearest to Allah are its mosques, and the parts most hateful to Allah are markets. Sahih Muslim 671*

It is highly desirable that a Muslim should spend his time in the market place only when it is necessary for him or her. Buying, selling, shopping for household items and food, and looking for things of personal use are not matters of concern. It becomes an undesirable action when a person roams about in the market place just to pass his or her time, or to spend his or her money unnecessarily in useless items.

Surah Al e Imran 141:

And be not excessive. Indeed, He does not like those who commit excess.

Surah Al Araf 31:

O children of Adam, take your adornment at every masjid, and eat and drink, but be not excessive. Indeed, He likes not those who commit excess.

Extravagance is discouraged in our beautiful way of life to maintain a healthy balance in the society. We are however encouraged to spend generously on the poor, needy, wayfarer and orphans and it bears immense rewards too! Allah does not burden us beyond our capacities so He asks His servants to spend from that which is extra out of their own expenses and need.

Surah Baqarah 215:

They ask you, [O Muhammad], what they should spend. Say, "Whatever you spend of good is [to be] for parents and relatives and orphans and the needy and the traveler. And whatever you do of good - indeed, Allah is Knowing of it."

Spending Time with Family

As mentioned earlier it is good for a Muslim to spend quality time with his family members. Enjoying, joking, playing, learning and traveling. This not only strengthens the bond of love among them but also helps in a rich and healthy lifestyle. In today's busy world with all the distractions at hand we find ourselves too occupied and overwhelmed with all the technology and social media websites. We must not forget that the first and foremost people who deserve our love, care, affection, help and attention are those who are the closest to us. Our family deserves all the best from us so that our home becomes a place where we find peace, comfort, enjoyment and where we feel free to be ourselves growing in our innate capabilities as well as the nurtured ones.

Being with a family is in itself a great blessing because there are many in the world who have lost their families in mishaps, wars and natural calamities. We must have a soft corner for those unfortunate ones in the world and be thankful if Allah has blessed us with a home, a family, a job and many other things that they might crave for.

Not forgetting those unfortunate relatives or strangers, the old, the poor and those in need. Helping them in whatever ways and means one can earn Allah's pleasure. Even if you find yourself unable to help them in any way substantial, you can just keep good relations with them by visiting them and keeping in touch with them. Never cut off relations just because they are not well off or unfortunate in any other way.

'Abdullah ibn 'Amr reported that the Prophet ﷺ said:
"The one who maintains ties of kinship is not the one who reciprocates. The one who maintains ties of kinship is the one who, when his relatives cut him off, maintains ties of kinship."
Sahih Al Albani

Praying

An inseparable part of a Muslim's daily routine is his or her obligatory prayers. Prayer is the only daily duty among the few obligatory duties that a Muslim is expected to perform in his life. This is so beautiful that no matter what a person is doing in his life, no matter how busy he is and no matter what his condition is; he is always in a connection with Allah.

Surah Al Baqarah 43:

And establish prayer and give zakah and bow with those who bow [in worship and obedience].

These daily prayers constantly remind him of the Creator and he humbles himself before him in prostration and finds peace and strength from his renewed Eman day by day. The prayers are not just an exercise rather they act as our daily meditation and reconnection with the Creator amidst numerous activities that we do in a routine life. Prayers give us the feeling of solace and comfort that we belong to our Lord and He is our Master and Guide. Performing the daily prayers always freshens up our mind and gives us a new energy to continue with our life again and again. The ablution performed before each prayer refreshes our physical as well as spiritual body because we know the rewards and benefits attached to it.

A Muslim does not deliberately miss his prayer. A Muslim man is best when he prayers his daily obligatory prayers in the mosque.

Narrated `Abdullah bin `Umar:

Allah's Messenger ﷺ said, "The prayer in congregation is twenty seven times superior to the prayer offered by person alone."

Sahih Al Bukhari 645

A Muslim woman can also offer the prayer in the mosque but it is better if she chooses the inside of her house for her worship. Going to the mosque for the prayers and the special Friday prayers is very rewarding in the eyes of Allah. Congregation instills discipline, unity, oneness and devotion to Allah in all the Muslims.

Jabir (May Allah be pleased with him) reported:

Messenger of Allah ﷺ said, "The five daily Salat (prayers) are like a great river running by your door in which you take a bath five times a day."
Muslim

Daily prayers keep many evils away from us as Allah says in Surah Al Ankabut 45:

Recite (O Muhammad SAW) what has been revealed to you of the Book (the Quran), and perform As-Salat (Iqamat-as-Salat). Verily, As-Salat (the prayer) prevents from Al-Fahsha' (i.e. great sins of every kind, unlawful sexual intercourse, etc.) and Al-Munkar (i.e. disbelief, polytheism, and every kind of evil wicked deed, etc.) and the remembering (praising, etc.) of (you by) Allah (in front of the angels) is greater indeed [than your remembering (praising, etc.) Allah in prayers, etc.]. And Allah knows what you do.

Making ablution keeps us clean physically as well as spiritually. As said by our dear Prophet, ablution and prayers shake off our sins from us just as a palm tree sheds its leaves and keep us clean as we are near a river bathing five times a day.

It is highly appreciated if a person dresses himself up properly for the mosque and is well groomed, clean and smelling good. Surah Al Araf 31 states:

> *O Seeds (Or: sons) of Adam! Take your adornment at every mosque, and eat and drink, and do not be extravagant; surely He does not love the extravagant.*

It is best for us to take our children to the Masjid from the very start when they have learned how to pray. When they are manageable and know the etiquettes of the houses of Allah we must instill in them the love of Praying in Congregation as this proves to be very useful for them. From this practice of daily attending the mosque children tend to spend their time in more important things in life, prioritizing their routine tasks according to their importance and learning punctuality, discipline and manners from an early age. In the company of the righteous they naturally learn many things which cannot be taught to them through schooling or education like maturity of thought, wisdom, good company, spending time in rewarding actions and contemplation.

Surah Al Araf 204 reads:

> *So when the Qur'an is recited, then listen to it and pay attention that you may receive mercy.*

They also learn patience and tolerance when they interact and socialize on a daily basis. Islam teaches community life and unity and cooperation within the society. Children learn to work as a team and feel as one whole body as Muslims.

Since we are talking of everyday Islam this part of our daily life is the most important to instill in ourselves and our children and to be steadfast on it so that in the end we become one strong Ummah which ensures easy and peaceful living not just for the Muslims but for the whole of mankind.

Socializing

It is an established fact that man is a social animal. Even our religion Islam, teaches us to be social and friendly to all. Islam discourages aloofness from society to attain sainthood or to devote all the time in worship. It is highly recommended that a Muslim meets the neighbors, keeps in touch with the fellow human beings, contacts friends and relatives on a regular basis and to reach out to the unfortunate ones.

Surah An Nisa 36 states:

Worship Allah and associate nothing with Him, and to parents do good, and to relatives, orphans, the needy, the near neighbor, the neighbor farther away, the companion at your side, the traveler, and those whom your right hands possess. Indeed, Allah does not like those who are self-deluding and boastful.

One must keep oneself informed of all the neighboring houses. It is considered very bad if one's neighbor is hungry and we are eating food without sharing it with him. Unlike the misconception we should be kind to all neighbors; Muslims or not.

Islam teaches kindness and sympathy not only to people but even to the animals. Also visiting the sick is a very noble work in the eyes of Almighty Allah.

Ibn 'Umar ﷺ and 'Aishah رضي الله عنها reported:

Messenger of Allah ﷺ said, "Jibril kept recommending treating neighbors with kindness until I thought he would assign a

share of inheritance".
Al-Bukhari and Muslim

It is reported on the authority of Abu Huraira that the Messenger of Allah ﷺ observed:

He who believes in Allah and the Last Day should either utter good words or better keep silence; and he who believes in Allah and the Last Day should treat his neighbor with kindness and he who believes in Allah and the Last Day should show hospitality to his guest.
Sahih Muslim 47

Having a good neighbor is important but being a good neighbor is highly rewarding! Note that it is not mentioned whether your neighbor is Muslim or not; if you have a neighbor he is entitled to your kindness. You are not supposed to hurt him by any means because this can cost you Jannah! According to one hadith:

Narrated by Abu Shuraih:

The Prophet ﷺ said, "By Allah, he does not believe! By Allah, he does not believe! By Allah, he does not believe!" It was said, "Who is that, O Allah's Messenger (ﷺ)?" He said, "That person whose neighbor does not feel safe from his evil."
Sahih Al Bukhari

Reading Quran and Contemplation

We spend most of our time earning our livelihood. Little do we realize that all that is with us is from Allah and all that we enjoy is nothing but Allah's blessing. We must take some time out to read the book that Allah ﷻ sent to our last Prophet (peace by upon him) and try to comprehend what Allah has ordered us to do in His Book. We must try to acquire more and more knowledge of our religion and not remain ignorant and unmindful of Allah's ﷻ commands.

The book of Allah ﷻ is a guide for those who fear Allah and want to take the straight path. This book has some rights on us as Muslims. We must read it with attention, listen to it when it is being recited in prayers or otherwise, try to know it's meaning and understand it and most importantly apply its teachings in our daily life.

When our love for Allah ﷻ and His Messenger ﷺ surpasses all the other things then we are able to give the due importance to the Words of Allah and the teachings of His Prophet. We must learn to recite the Book of Allah with correct recitation method which is referred to as Tajweed. We must read and understand Quran on a daily basis.

After we have built a good connection with this living miracle and an amazing manual from Allah sent for our guidance, it is our duty to pass it on to others as well. Here too we start with our family first. Teaching our spouse and children the Book of Allah and its manners and etiquettes and its rights upon us, will earn us huge rewards for this world as well as the next. Quran should be a part of our daily life routine. Reciting it in prayers is something we already do but reciting directly from the Book is also very important.

Narrated Abu Musa:

The Prophet ﷺ said, "Keep on reciting the Qur'an, for, by Him in Whose Hand my life is, Qur'an runs away (is forgotten) faster than camels that are released from their tying ropes."
Sahih Bukhari 5033

At this point we must know that at the same time we also believe in the earlier scriptures sent by Allah to the other Prophets and their people. We believe in all those books because Allah ﷻ sent the Quran as a proof for those books and as a final commandment to be followed by all.

Surah Al Baqarah 4 declares:

And who believe in (the Quran and the Sunnah) which has been sent down (revealed) to you (Muhammad Peace be upon him) and in [the Taurat (Torah) and the Injeel (Gospel), etc.] which were sent down before you and they believe with certainty in the Hereafter. (Resurrection, recompense of their good and bad deeds, Paradise and Hell, etc.).

The Month of Fasting

The month of Fasting is the most beneficial month for the Muslims. This month is capable of wiping off all our sins if we fast and worship properly and sincerely. After this month Muslims celebrate Eid as a festival. One must thank Allah, for giving us such moments of happiness and chances to earn rewards. In these happy moments we must thank Allah and never forget the needy and the poor.

Surah Al Baqarah 185 states:

The month of Ramadhan [is that] in which was revealed the Qur'an, a guidance for the people and clear proofs of guidance and criterion. So whoever sights [the new moon of] the month, let him fast it; and whoever is ill or on a journey - then an equal number of other days. Allah intends for you ease and does not intend for you hardship and [wants] for you to complete the period and to glorify Allah for that [to] which He has guided you; and perhaps you will be grateful.

The month of Ramadan is undoubtedly a month of great opportunity to revitalize our eman (faith), to boost our energy, to enhance our goodness, to get our sins forgiven, to attain greater levels in Taqwa (fear of Allah), to learn to tame our desires, to have a renewed balanced lifestyle with a check on our diet, sleeping patterns and most importantly the spiritual aspect of our life as a Muslim.

Ramadan not only instills a greater spirit of thankfulness and gratitude toward Allah but it also gets us genuinely closer to Him and His Book the Quran. There is something special about this month. All over the world Muslims experience the uniqueness of this Blessed month in their own way. Some take this month as a spiritual training to become better Muslims and feel that during and after Ramadan their love for Allah and His Deen (Way of Life) has increased and renewed.

This month comes with an annual plan and training project for the whole of Muslim community. Everyone feels the love for this month as they fast just for the sake of Allah and out of no compulsion. Allah loves His servants as they control their desires for His sake and He promises rewards for those who fast.

Abu Hurairah narrated that:

The Messenger of Allah ﷺ said: "Indeed your Lord said: 'Every good deed is rewarded with ten of the same up to seven hundred times over. Fasting is for Me, and I shall reward for it.' Fasting is a shield from the Fire. The smell coming from the mouth of the one fasting is more pleasant to Allah than the scent of musk. If one of you is abused by an ignorant person while fasting, then let him say: 'Indeed I am fasting.'" Sahih Jami at Tirmidhi

The Month of Hajj

The month of Hajj is also of great importance. Those Muslims who have all the means to perform Hajj must not delay it for any reason. Performing Hajj free of all vices brings out man as a newborn without any blemish of sin. It is obligatory once in a lifetime.

It was narrated from Abu Hurairah that the Prophet ﷺ said:

"From one 'Umrah to another is an expiation for the sins that came in between them, and Hajj Mabrur (an accepted Hajj) brings no less a reward than Paradise."
Sunan Ibn Majah Sahih

Surah Al Baqarah 196 reads:

And complete the Hajj and 'umrah for Allah. But if you are prevented, then [offer] what can be obtained with ease of sacrificial animals. And do not shave your heads until the sacrificial animal has reached its place of slaughter. And whoever among you is ill or has an ailment of the head [making shaving necessary must offer] a ransom of fasting [three days] or charity or sacrifice. And when you are secure, then whoever performs 'umrah [during the Hajj months] followed by Hajj [offers] what can be obtained with ease of sacrificial animals. And whoever cannot find [or afford such an animal] - then a fast of three days during Hajj and of seven when you have returned [home]. Those are ten complete [days]. This is for those whose family is not in the area of al-Masjid al-Haram. And fear Allah and know that Allah is severe in penalty.

Hajj is not just a ritual but a very comprehensive training of a lifetime. A pilgrim has to go through a variety of things for completing Hajj. The journey is simple but it demands a lot of patience to perform all the duties that it contains. A pilgrim learns a lot of things in this journey. First he has to settle all his affairs as he intends to go for the journey of a lifetime. He has to plan for it and gain information about the correct way to perform it so that out of ignorance is does not lose the reward which is promised.

The pilgrim sets out for hajj with the things that he might need while he is on the journey and the best thing he takes with him is the fear of Allah ﷺ. He has to be adorned with taqwa so that whatever situation he encounters is dealt with keeping in mind the rewards of Hajj and that it is just for the sake of Allah ﷺ. A pilgrim can suffer difficulties while he performs all the duties of Hajj as he stays with lot of people from different backgrounds he has to always practice patience and forbearance. During Hajj we are away from home and do not get all the facilities that we enjoy and all the rest that we take there. Hajj demands constancy, perseverance, patience and the will to do it without engaging in foul, useless, vulgar and indecent talks and actions. A pilgrim should be extra careful not to fall into dispute with anyone and not to indulge in anything that might be undesirable in the eyes of Allah ﷺ.

Surah Al Baqarah 197 states:
Hajj is [during] well-known months, so whoever has made Hajj obligatory upon himself therein [by entering the state of ihram], there is [to be for him] no sexual relations and no disobedience and no disputing during Hajj. And whatever good you do - Allah knows it. And take provisions, but indeed, the best provision is fear of Allah . And fear Me, O you of understanding.

Each one of us desires to fulfill this duty of Hajj because it is obligatory upon us only once in a lifetime but it holds immense reward. Surah Al e Imran 96-97 declares:

Indeed, the first House [of worship] established for mankind was that at Makkah - blessed and a guidance for the worlds.

In it are clear signs [such as] the standing place of Abraham. And whoever enters it shall be safe. And [due] to Allah from the people is a pilgrimage to the House - for whoever is able to find thereto a way. But whoever disbelieves - then indeed, Allah is free from need of the worlds.

And Surah Al Haj 27 reads:

And proclaim to the people the Hajj [pilgrimage]; they will come to you on foot and on every lean camel; they will come from every distant pass.

Hence Hajj can be a complete turner of hearts and a great source of reward if it is done with the sole intention of pleasing Allah ﷻ and obeying His command. Apart from all these usual activities a Muslim goes through phases like education, job, marriage, child rearing, taking care of old parents, and no doubt some hard times in life.

Seeking Education

While seeking education one must be sincere and devoted as an educated Muslim is far better than an ignorant one. Surah Luqman 20 states:

> Do you not see that Allah has made subject to you whatever is in the heavens and whatever is in the earth and amply bestowed upon you His favors, [both] apparent and unapparent? But of the people is he who disputes about Allah without knowledge or guidance or an enlightening Book [from Him].

It is best to be well informed and well equipped. We must realize that we acquire education to help ourselves and others around us. Good educated Muslims will definitely build a better community than non-serious and idle Muslims. The aim of education should be to seek knowledge and to develop the knowhow of the current system so as to build a respectable place in the world and not just to earn money and fame. We should know this for sure that the source of all knowledge is none but Allah. The important thing in the pursuit of knowledge is not going just for the trends and contemporary areas but to seek the truth and wisdom which is the underlying source of every field.

It was narrated from Jabir that:

> The Messenger of Allah ﷺ said: "Ask Allah for beneficial knowledge and seek refuge with Allah from knowledge that is of no benefit."
> Sunan Ibn Majah Hasan

Many times it happens that we just react and respond to the information around us without verifying it. As this is a phase where there is information overload and you can gain access to almost anything on the electronic media, there's a genuine need for something that can keep us rooted and equipped with something which is authentic, true, free of doubt and contradiction and totally reliable. That is none other than the Quran, the Book of Allah, the One and Only God; the Source of all that exists and the source of all knowledge and wisdom. Surah Al Baqarah 32 declares:

> They said, "Exalted are You; we have no knowledge except what You have taught us. Indeed, it is You who is the Knowing, the Wise."

When we read the Quran we realize that it not only addresses the issues of the people that have gone past but it successfully tackles the issues of modern times. We have the belief that it is a Book in which there is no doubt. As stated in Quran itself in Surah Al Baqarah 2:

> This is the Book about which there is no doubt, a guidance for those conscious of Allah

Once we have the knowledge and qualification we can opt for the best jobs that are suitable for us. This paves way for us to help out others in our own way. When we are well established and have access to the needful we can help those who need us to seek knowledge, job or help of any kind. Apart from this we first of all help our nation by being a good employee.

The intention of seeking knowledge should be to earn the pleasure of Allah the Creator of all that exists and His pleasure lies in being good to His Creation. The best among us are those who are the most beneficial to others.

Among the other things that we can do to be beneficial to others is to teach them whatever we learn. Sharing knowledge is encouraged and highly rewarding in Islam. According to one Hadith:

> Narrated `Uthman:
>
> *The Prophet ﷺ said, "The best among you (Muslims) are those who learn the Qur'an and teach it." Sahih Bukhari*

Knowledge is acquired for various purposes and the most common is to earn a living. It is not bad to learn things and to earn a living out of it but this should not be the ultimate aim in life. Life is temporary and whatever in it is temporary. We shall go away but our legacy with linger behind in the form of what we shared with others, what we benefitted them with and what we gave them in the form of knowledge and wisdom.

A Muslim's goal is not limited to this world but he thinks simultaneously to earn his place in Jannah and to earn the pleasure of Allah ﷻ. According to another hadith we know that worldly gain should not be the sole intention behind seeking knowledge. A believer is mindful of the fact that whatever he acquires is because of the Mercy and Grace of His Lord, so he does not forget the pleasure of his Maker in any act that he carries out.

> Abu Hurairah ؓ reported:
>
> *The Messenger of Allah ﷺ said, "He who does not acquire knowledge with the sole intention of seeking the Pleasure of Allah but for worldly gain, will not smell the fragrance of Jannah on the Day of Resurrection."*
> Abu Dawud

Marriage

Marrying is a sunnah of our beloved Prophet Muhammad ﷺ. He encouraged the youth to get married. It was narrated from Aishah that:

> The Messenger of Allah said: "Marriage is part of my sunnah, and whoever does not follow my sunnah has nothing to do with me. Get married, for I will boast of your great numbers before the nations. Whoever has the means, let him get married, and whoever does not, then he should fast for it will diminish his desire." Sunan Ibn Majah Hasan

The practical implication of this tradition is that the society needs a legal and healthy unit of family relationships that build a whole community and contribute toward an overall strong environment with values. Such an environment nurtures children who become the torch bearers of Islamic ethics and ideology.

Marriage is not a matter of jest. It is a matter which involves an important decision to be taken for your life. It is something you decide to live for the rest of your life. The person you choose to marry is the one who will be with you day and night and will be a part of your routine life.

Hence, the decision to get married should not be done in haste. It should be done with wisdom and poise and with the consent and counsel of the bride, the groom, their guardians and witnesses. This ensures a better foundation for a lifelong relationship Allah willing. Also, before or after taking the decision to send the proposal it is better if one prays the Istikhara prayer which is the best counsel one can seek in any important matter; the counsel of Allah. After that one can go about taking action in that matter and trust Allah ﷻ and leave things in His care.

The Istikhara prayer is as stated in the hadith below:

Jabir bin Abdullah narrated:
"Allah's Messenger would teach us Al-Isthikhara for all of our affairs just as he would teach us a Surah of the Qur'an, saying: 'When one of you is worried about a matter, then let him perform two Rak'ah other than the obligatory (prayer), then let him say: (Allahumma inni astakhiruka bi'ilmika, wa astaqdiruka biqudratika, wa as'aluka min falikal-azim, fa innaka taqdiru wa la qadiru, wa ta'lami wa la a'lamu, wa anta allamul-ghayub. Allahumma in kunta ta'lamu anna hadhal-amra khairun li fi dini wa ma'ishati wa aqibati amri, or said: Fi ajili amri wa ajilihi fayassirhu li,thumma barik li fihi, wa in kunta ta'lamu anna hadhal-amra sharrun li fi dini wa ma'ishati wa aqibati amri, or said: Fi ajili amri wa ajilihi fasrifhu anni wasrifni anhu waqdur Lil-khaira haithu kana, thumma ardini bih.)" 'O Allah! I consult Your knowledge, and seek ability from Your power, and I ask You from Your magnificent bounty, for indeed You have power and I do not have power, and You know while I do not know, and You know the unseen. O Allah! If you know that this matter is good for me in my religion or my livelihood, and for my life in the Hereafter - or he said: for my present and future - then make it easy for me, then bless me in it. If You know that this matter is bad for me in my religion and my livelihood and my life in the Hereafter - or he said: for my present and future - then divert it from me and divert me from it, enable me to find the good wherever it is, then make me pleased with it." He said: "And he mentions his need."
Sahih Jami at Tirmidhi

Marrying someone for piety is the best option as this will be lasting as compared to their beauty or wealth which might give you pleasure and benefit for some time but can leave you at a point of time. Choosing a life partner is also very important in our life. We must choose the one who is a good Muslim or Muslimah.

It is encouraged to look for a spouse who is well placed according to the Deen and abides by the duties of Allah. The character and values of a person are more enduring than the physical attributes and financial status.

Narrated Abu Hurairah:

> *It was narrated from Abu Hurairah that the Prophet said: "Women are married for four things: their wealth, their nobility, their beauty and their religious commitment. Choose the one who is religiously committed, may your hands be rubbed with dust."*
> Sahih Sunan An Nisai

Therefore, in Islam it is highly recommended to marry and that too marry for a higher purpose; to build a strong Ummah and to contribute toward providing the world with healthy, God-fearing and good Muslims.

Sometimes it is not easy for some youth to get married at the desired age and this is indeed a big test for them. As we are not left unguided in any matter by Allah ﷻ we have something for this scenario as well:

> Narrated 'Alqama:
> *While I was walking with `Abdullah he said, "We were in the company of the Prophet ﷺ and he said, 'He who can afford to marry should marry, because it will help him refrain from looking at other women, and save his private parts from committing illegal sexual relation; and he who cannot afford*

to marry is advised to fast, as fasting will diminish his sexual power."
Sahih al Bukhari

We can very well see how Islam is all for a healthy and pure environment and demands that its followers be the ones who ensure establishing such a world which is cleaner, purer and safer for our youth and children. The phase today is witnessing a lot of turmoil where rape, disrespect of women and illegal relationships are on the rise daily. Surah Baqarah 268 declares:

> Satan threatens you with poverty and orders you to immorality, while Allah promises you forgiveness from Him and bounty. And Allah is all-Encompassing and Knowing.

A good person and a good citizen will never want such a society to thrive, and to eventually destroy all values and bonds of kinship and family. The enemies of mankind often desire a free society where they are not questioned about anything and where they are left to do whatever their animal instincts instruct them to do.

Surah Al Baqarah 169 reads:

> Tells us what Satan instructs us to do: He only orders you to evil and immorality and to say about Allah what you do not know.

This is highly abominable and discouraged as it is a threat to the physical and spiritual health of every being. It is abiding on every Muslim, hence, to follow the teachings of Islam to shape his life in the best manner.

Surah An Nahl 90 declares:
Indeed, Allah orders justice and good conduct and giving to relatives and forbids immorality and bad conduct and oppression. He admonishes you that perhaps you will be reminded.

It is not just a matter of five daily prayers or the other pillars of Islam but it is a routine matter which cannot be ignored even in our daily life. We are not Muslims only when we attend a prayer in the mosque or fast in Ramadan. We are Muslims every moment of our life. We have to live, act, breathe and die as Muslims.

The life of a Muslim as understood by all the commandments of Allah ﷻ and the duties that He has assigned to us is not specific to situations but it is every moment of life. If we consider the life from the day of our birth to the last day in this world we find that each moment has the connection with the Islamic lifestyle. There are teachings on the birth of a baby where we are taught even what to give her to eat just after birth!

Parenting or Child rearing

Marriage in Islam is a union of two persons for the increase of believers and righteous men and women in the Ummah. This is the responsibility of the parents to bring up such children who grow up to become pious Muslims. The children we rear at home are the building blocks of the society. It is extremely important for the parents to be just and responsible with the kids from the very start. We must never neglect them in any phase of life.

Narrated Abu Hurairah:

The Messenger of Allah ﷺ as saying: When a man dies, his action discontinues from him except three things, namely, perpetual sadaqah (charity), or the knowledge by which benefit is acquired, or a pious child who prays for him. Sahih Al Albani

We should be very careful with respect to their habits and manners. It is fruitful to get them used to good habits from the very start and let them witness those in us first which is the best way of teaching them anything. Good habits are with us always if they are instilled in us from our childhood because then they become our second nature and we do them very easily and comfortably.

Childrearing, hence, is a very responsible thing to do for the parents. They need to be well informed and sensible in order to rear their children in the best way. Today it is even a bigger and more difficult a challenge to take care of kids and give them quality time and good attention. There is so much to spoil them and so much to distract them that it is an even greater responsibility to keep a check on what they are spending time with. Whatever they see, watch, read or come in contact with undoubtedly leave an impact on the child's mind.

Parents must act like mature and sensitive beings so as to be able to shape the soft and brittle personality of an innocent child. Children learn more from the atmosphere of home than from educational institutes and books. A mother's lap is said to be the first school for the children to learn their practical lessons.

Whatever work we are doing is no longer important when our child needs our attention except our duty to our Lord.

During prayers too mothers can hold their child if she is scared or crying too much.

Narrated Abdullah ibn Amr ibn al-'As:

> *The Messenger of Allah ﷺ said: Command your children to pray when they become seven years old, and beat them for it (prayer) when they become ten years old; and arrange their beds (to sleep) separately.*
>
> Hasan Sahih Al Al bani

The Muslim father is rewarded even for what is his duty and what he seemingly does in a routine manner. If he comes to know that whatever he does for his family amounts up to charity, one of the most desirable actions, he would feel more and more inclined to love, take care of and feel responsible about his family.

According to one hadith as narrated by Abu Mas'ud Al-Ansari:

> *The Prophet ﷺ said, "When a Muslim spends something on his family intending to receive Allah's reward it is regarded as Sadaqa for him."*
>
> Sahih Al Bukhari 5351

Therefore Muslim parents must take extra care to look after the educational, spiritual and physical growth of their children and make them such that even after they are gone their children become sadqa e jariya or ongoing charity for them.

Only righteous children will care about supplicating for the parents and doing acts of kindness to benefit others.

Taking Care of Parents

Taking care of parents is a duty upon every child. This too comes in a daily routine because caring on some occasion as birthdays, Mother's Day, Father's Day or any other day does not do the needful. We should be sensible enough to give them our time, attention and care all the time. Even if we are too busy we can do things like fixing up some time to visit them daily or if they live far away we can plan to visit them weekly or monthly. If this too is not possible we can make it a point to keep in touch with them and their needs through various channels like phone and emails. It is greatly important to fulfill this duty as it has been emphasized time and again in the Quran as well as in the hadith.

Abdullah bin Amr narrated that:

The Prophet said: "The Lord's pleasure is in the parent's pleasure, and the Lord's anger is in the parent's anger." Jami at Tirmidhi (Hasan).

Today, the sad truth is that neither parents are acting as responsible adults nor the children are coming out to be obedient and God-fearing. The reason is not so much in the happenings of this era but more on the outlook we have adopted toward the life, the world, the Deen of Islam as a whole. Islam was completed as a religion and Deen which Allah ﷻ has chosen for us. It is neither outdated nor does it need to be molded according to the changing scenes. It is a misconception that since world has changed so much and has witnessed such great revolutions and advancements we need to reconsider the ways we can adjust Islam according to our liking and fancy.

This is heart breaking and sad. The only solution is adhering to the teachings of the Quran and taking examples from authentic ahadith. The correct knowledge and a lot of sincere prayers can keep us on the right path and save us from wavering. Allah ﷻ has put great emphasis on the care of parents and we can find this in the Quran in Surah An Nisa 36:

> *Worship Allah and associate nothing with Him, and to parents do good, and to relatives, orphans, the needy, the near neighbor, the neighbor farther away, the companion at your side, the traveler, and those whom your right hands possess. Indeed, Allah does not like those who are self-deluding and boastful.*

It is a thing to be noted and worth a thought that Allah ﷻ mentions being good to our parents right after His worship. This is commonly known that mothers have paradise under their feet and that mothers are three times more entitled to our kindness compared to fathers. Mothers and fathers both are our benefactors, caretakers, encouragers, guides and supporters. There are numerous kids all over the world who are deprived of the blessing of one or both of their parents due to some or the other reason. It should be considered no less than a great blessing to have one or both of your parents under your care or to have yourself under their supervision.

Orphans have a difficult life at their disposal. When they do not have a father to look after them their mothers have a tough time looking after them. They are forced to be under other people's care and are totally dependent on others for life's basic needs if they happen to be poor. It is highly recommended to be very kind to the orphans because they go through lots of emotional and financial hardships.

If one wants to realize the importance of parents one should think about the orphans for a while and if possible visit such places where he can find them. This will bring softness and kindness into his heart and his love and value for his parents will increase manifold.

A family is a unit of parents and children. It does not matter if the children have grown up and started earning their living and the parents have grown old and retired from their jobs. This is the very time when the children are more likely to take care of their old parents and this is the time when they are in need of their attention and care the most.

It is reported on the authority of 'Abdullah that the Messenger of Allah ﷺ observed:

The best of the deeds or deed is the (observance of) prayer at its proper time and kindness to the parents. Sahih Muslim 85

Difficulties and Troubles

Surah Al Baqarah 155 declares:
And We will surely test you with something of fear and hunger and a loss of wealth and lives and fruits, but give good tidings to the patient...

And in Surah Muhammad 31:
And We will surely test you until We make evident those who strive among you [for the cause of Allah] and the patient, and We will test your affairs.

As Muslims we must be clear in this regard that we have been created for test. Whatever situation we are put into is actually a test for us, be it good or bad. The good situation is a test of our loyalty and thankfulness to Allah ﷻ and our behavior during that happy state. When a person is granted riches it is not something that we think a Muslim should feel guilty about rather he should be greatly thankful that Allah ﷻ has given him so much and now he is able to spend his assets for the sake of Allah in various acts of charity and welfare. He can become a great source of help to the poor in the society and can contribute heartily to the projects running for the benefit of poor and needy.

Surah Al Baqarah 215 reads:

They ask you, [O Muhammad], what they should spend. Say, "Whatever you spend of good is [to be] for parents and relatives and orphans and the needy and the traveler. And whatever you do of good - indeed, Allah is Knowing of it."

He can utilize his wealth in numerous other things like building of hospitals, orphanages, masajids, schools and religious schools for the community. Here I would like to clarify that Muslims wrongly feel that their halal wealth can be utilized only for the Muslims and for the organizations run by them. This is not the case. It is recommended that we spend our wealth for the betterment of the society as a whole and not everywhere we can find a completely Muslim society. We do want to be responsible citizens and countrymen. It is our responsibility to contribute in the ongoing charity programs run by Muslims and non-Muslims alike.

The outlook of a Muslim who is well informed, educated and strongly connected to the Quran and Sunnah is not constricted. He is very open minded and large hearted. He is kind to all of Mankind.

A Muslim's affair is all good. When good touches him he is thankful and when something bad happens he is patient. Allah ﷻ rewards us in every situation that is hard on us, even for a prick of thorn. Suhaib reported that Allah's Messenger ﷺ said:

> Strange are the ways of a believer for there is good in every affair of his and this is not the case with anyone else except in the case of a believer for if he has an occasion to feel delight, he thanks (God), thus there is a good for him in it, and if he gets into trouble and shows resignation (and endures it patiently), there is a good for him in it.
> Sahih Muslim 2999

How Merciful is Allah ﷻ! When troubles come we should not forget everything and start lamenting rather we must at once remind ourselves that it is indeed a test from Allah and we have to pass it in flying colors. No situation good or bad lasts forever. We need to be aware of what Allah ﷻ has asked us to do at times of distress and difficulties and practice that as true believers. Surah Al Baqarah 45 says:

> And seek help through patience and prayer, and indeed, it is difficult except for the humbly submissive [to Allah]

Enjoining Good and Forbidding Evil

The Holy Quran declares in Surah At Tawbah 71:

> The believing men and believing women are allies of one another. They enjoin what is right and forbid what is wrong and establish prayer and give zakah and obey Allah and His Messenger. Those Allah will have mercy upon them. Indeed, Allah is Exalted in Might and Wise.

This is one duty which is not being taken seriously by us. Allah ﷻ tells us so clearly that 'believing men and believing women' are helpers, supporters, allies of each other. They have a bond in terms of their faith. They are responsible for the betterment of each other. This command of Allah if followed properly will become such a great source of bringing back the lost glory and unity of the Muslim Ummah. We have divided in terms of sects and ideologies but this has only resulted in the decline of the greatness of our own identity as Muslims.

We must be united in terms of just one Faith, the faith of Ibrahim عَلَيْهِ ٱلسَّلَامُ, Musa عَلَيْهِ ٱلسَّلَامُ, Isa عَلَيْهِ ٱلسَّلَامُ and Muhammad ﷺ. The thing that is mentioned here is enjoining good and forbidding evil. This too has its implications directly into our daily routine. Don't we interact with so many people on a daily basis? We do. Don't we get into situations where we see something being done utterly wrong? We do. Don't we as parents, friends, colleagues and neighbors find things which should be shared with others and should be told to our loved ones so that they too benefit from it? There is no need for creating any platform for doing such things on a daily basis.

If we are praying on time we can just call out to others and remind them too. If we are planning to spend in charity for some particular poor family we can ask others to join us in this noble venture. We can invite our friends over if we are attending some dawah lecture or conference. When we see our loved ones engaged in some irresponsible behavior or bad thing we can politely stop them and advise them to mend their ways in a wise way. This is not all. On a daily basis most of us come in contact with various unhealthy information and fake news circulating in the social media and among social groups. We can take some extra effort and do some research to find out the truth and let others know about the reality saving them from falling into the trap of false information and rumors.

All this and much more comprise of the ways we can enjoin good and forbid evil for others and earn the great reward of pleasing Allah ﷻ by obeying His clear commands in the Quran.

Propagation of Islam

There's no wondering that how the propagation of Islam can be something of a routine nature. Yes, it can be. We are Muslims and we practice Islam in our life. We go about doing our work to many places and as a result we meet many people.

The first group of people we come in contact is none other than our family. Propagating Islam is not just for the non-Muslims but it starts right from the home. It starts from our own self first. We should discipline ourselves as good Muslims and train ourselves into making our habits of a good Muslim stronger each day by doing them religiously. We can make it a habit to pray on time which is the most liked deed by Allah ﷻ.

We can show our children how to be kind to parents by being kind to our parents first. Children learn what they see. No amount of lecture can work like the work of a silent deed done to show what you believe in. Reciting the Quran and trying to understand it at home can also instill the same thing in the other members. Starting from home we can propagate Islam to our non-Muslim neighbors by being kind and pleasant to them. We should make them feel that we are always there for their help if ever they need us. Good manners and kindness has urged many non-Muslims to know more about the otherwise distorted image of Muslims and Islam as a whole. Many have shown interest in learning the religion of Islam only after witnessing the way a child looks after his parents or a husband protecting a wife, or by noticing how disciplined the Muslims are in terms of their prayers, charity and cleanliness.

Propagation of our Deen can be done is a more structured and planned out manner as well. We should be equipped with enough knowledge of our Deen so that we can answer the doubts that come up in the minds of those seeking the truth. Pamphlets can be distributed and books can be written and in today's advanced era electronic media can be utilized for this noble cause to reach people far and wide. Surah Al Muminun 73 declares:

And indeed, you invite them to a straight path.

While calling others to our Faith we should not be rude and we must never belittle their belief system. We just need to reach out to them and present the teachings of Islam in a pleasant manner and leave them to ponder over it themselves. It is indeed not upon us to bring anyone to the straight path. It is Allah ﷻ who guides.

Surah Yunus 25 states:

And Allah invites to the Home of Peace and guides whom He wills to a straight path

Summary

This brings us to the end of our daily duties and responsibilities as Muslims and as the torch bearers of the teachings of Quran and Allah's Messenger Muhammad ﷺ. Every day is indeed a new chapter in our life. Every day we need to do things that describe us silently as being the followers of certain lifestyle. This is the reason why we need to live Islam in our daily lives.

We cannot afford to say that today we are not feeling like doing something just out of laziness or carelessness. Muslims can always be aware and conscious of their identity as the followers of Islam when they remain in constant touch with the building blocks of their Faith and the source of their strength of Iman; and these are just the two things the Knowledge of Quran and Hadith.

We should always keep ourselves in touch with the Quran, read it, understand it and teach it to others. We must always establish our daily prayers and try to follow the little sunnahs of our beloved Prophet peace be upon him with utmost love and interest and instill the love of Quran, Sunnah and prayers in our children as well. Loving Islam is living Islam on a routine and daily basis; on an everyday basis. This ensures an easy and peaceful way of life for everyone, Allah Willing.

سبحانك اللهم و بحمدك أشهد أن لا إله إلا أنت أستغفرك و أتوب إليك *Subhaanak allaahumma wa bihamdika ash hadu an laa ilaaha illa anta astaghfiruka. Wa atubu ilayk* Glory be to You, O Allah! And Your Praise I bear witness that there is No God but You and I Seek Forgiveness from You and turn Toward you in Repentance

Shumaysa Amatul Hadi Faruqi

Glossary of Terms

ﷻ: Glory is His Majesty.

ﺭﺿﻲ ﺍﻟﻠﻪ ﻋﻨﻪ : Arabic for Radi'allahu ahnu which means may Allah be pleased with him/her and which is used after the companions of the prophet are mentioned.

ﷺ: Arabic for Salli'allahu alaiyhi wa'salaam which means may the peace and blessings of Allah be upon him and which is used after the a Prophet is mentioned.

عَلَيْهِ أَلسَّلَامُ: Arabic for ʿalayhi s-salām which means Peace be upon him

Barakah: Blessings
Bismillah: In the name of Allah
In shaa'Allah: if God wills; if God permits.
Taqwa: God consciousness. It has many further understandings and interpretations. Taqwa may mean piousness, fear of Allah, love for Allah, and self-restraint.
Wudhu: the ritual washing before prayers.
Miswak or Siwak: a toothbrush or stick of wood used to clean teeth. It has been proved that this stick has excellent benefits for human body.

Bibliography

The Holy Quran, English Translation of the meanings and commentary, Revised and Edited by The Presidency of Islamic Researchers (IFTA)

The Daily Life of the Prophet Muhammad, Dr. Syed Qudratullah Qadri Husami

Online References:
www.sunnah.com

About the Author

Shumaysa Amatul Hadi Faruqi is a student of Al Quran and a qualified Special Educator and Psychologist with a Master's degree from Jamia Millia Islamia. Her interests include reading, writing, researching and painting. She is an avid blogger and writes regularly at

http://www.shumaysafaruqi.blogspot.com

Book Summary

Everyday Islam: An Easy And Peaceful Way Of Life takes the reader from the very start of the day and through the possible situations and interactions that may occur with the words of Allah ﷻ and the example of His Messenger ﷺ. Shumaysa Amatul Hadi Faruqi utilizes the translations of the Holy Quran and the authentic Hadeeth to emphasize the importance of practicing and implementing the teachings of Islam in our daily lives. Islam is beautiful and its wisdom is for our benefit and success, in this life and the next. A Muslim submits himself to Allah ﷻ and thus adopts Islam as part of his or her identity while making right conduct a priority in every situation. To this end, **Everyday Islam** seeks to provide a source of reference for the busy, modern Muslim man and woman in keeping Islam active in their lives.

www.ingramcontent.com/pod-product-compliance
Lightning Source LLC
Chambersburg PA
CBHW032135090426
42743CB00007B/598